The *Help-Yourself* Book to Life, Health, & Happiness

In this Book, you will find all the Answers to Everything You Should Have Known but Didn't…

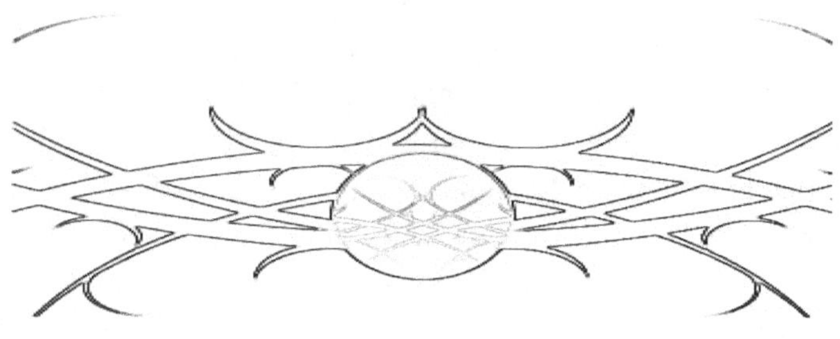

"…A Single Moment of Understanding Can Flood a Whole Life With Meaning." – Unknown

The Help-Youself Book to Life, Health, & Happiness
LCCN: 2010905127
ISBN: 978-0-615-36706-4
Non-Fiction, Adult, Young Adult, Reference
Published By: Nishan A. Kumaraperu

WWW.HELPYOURSELFBOOK.COM

The Help-Yourself Book to Life, Health, and Happiness:

SUMMARY: Do you have high Triglycerides & Cholesterol Problems? Find out how to lower your levels naturally with no side effects or Statin Drugs! Are you a Migraine sufferer? With this simple herb, reduce them by up to75%! Are you purchasing a new vehicle soon? Find out how to get the best deal possible and avoid the scams! Would you like to lose weight quickly & naturally? This supplement triples your metabolism! Are you a new homebuyer? We will give you the secrets to buy your home for the right price! In this book, you will find answers to all this and more…

Thank you for purchasing the Help Yourself book. Inside, you will find much of the knowledge I have accumulated over the past 15 years. I have made it a point to pass on a lot of this to family and friends who have made use of the beneficial information that is in here. I'm hoping that it will be just as important to the general public.

This information has been obtained in a variety of ways: Experimentation, Public Knowledge, Research, and Know-how. For some of you, this book may very well save your life & is well worth sharing. Enjoy the read and I hope this book will have a great impact on your life.

CHAPTER 1

THE MANY BENEFITS OF HERBAL ALTERNATIVES:

Herbal/Natural Remedies:

The benefits of Herbal Alternatives differ based on each Individual's bodily and genetic structure. This is the reason you hear that some things have worked for some people, while others have not. Each person is biologically different than the other, which can lead to beneficial effects or none at all. There is also a possibility of different reactions to Herbs based on various mixes with prescription drugs. Please consult your doctor before you take or mix any herbal supplement with a prescription drug or other supplements or consider taking as a daily regimen.

** Some of the following supplements may not be classified as 'Herbs', but will be listed in this section. Please remember that these are my suggestions because they have worked for me.

Probiotics: (Acidipholus, Lactobacillus, Bifidus)

The theory behind probiotics is interesting. Some say that most infections, colds, flus, etc. start in your digestive tract & work themselves up through your body from there. Your digestive tract consists of both good and bad bacteria, which in turn perform a number of metabolic activities. Bacteria as you know, multiplies at an alarming rate. If you can **replace the bad**

bacteria with good bacteria, this considerably lessens the chances of becoming sick.

Probiotics are naturally found in dairy products, such as milk, cheese, and yogurt. Unfortunately, these food products are pasteurized, killing **both** the bad and beneficial bacteria. There are products out there that now have Probiotics added to them, however rarely enough to make a difference. This bacteria is measured in the billions and a recommended dosage that can address existing imbalances is usually 10 billion or more live cultures.

From birth, my son had ear infections on a consistent basis; in fact – once a week. We tried everything: feeding him upright; keeping his ears warm & dry; even tubes. Nothing worked and after 2 sets of tubes, we just didn't know what to do anymore. The Doctor just kept saying that he had a bad Immune System and that 'he should grow out of it'.

Luckily for me, my neighbor was an Environmental Engineer and tutored me in the amazing properties of Probiotics. At age 3, I began giving my son an Acidopholus supplement in liquid form, twice a day. His periodic ear infections waned in less two months of supplementation. He is now 13 years old and has had 2-3 ear infections in the last 8 years!

A Probiotic supplement can:

- Help prevent infections of Intestinal Bugs
- Aid in Digestion
- Control vaginal PH

- Improve general immune system function
- Lower total and LDL Cholesterol
- Increase digestion of foods
- Reduce yeast infection, candidasis, and vaginitis
- Increase the assimilation of nutrients
- Promote anti-cancer activity in the body

Feverfew:

This is a natural herb that can lessen the frequency and pain associated with migraine headaches. I have friends who have had amazing success with this wonderful herb. If you are a migraine sufferer, 100-200mg of Feverfew a day will do wonders for you. It can also:

- Help relieve Arthritis, Fevers, Menstrual Problems, & Muscle Tension/Pain
- Lower Blood Pressure
- Improve Digestion/Stimulate Appetite
- Help with Stomach Irritation

Policosanol:

If you are like me or the many millions of Americans who eat a terrible diet of high-fat, artery-clogging foods, then this will be some great news for you! Policosanol is a derivative of sugar cane so it is glycol-based and sticks to the fats in your blood (Triglycerides). It has also been shown to exert a direct effect on the liver cells that control cholesterol manufacturing. As low a dose as 10mg per day could reduce total cholesterol by 16%+, LDL's by 24%, and increase HDL's by 29%! Other benefits include:

- Reducing the stickiness of blood platelets to prevent clotting
- Improves blood lipids
- Improves circulation and helps leg muscle pains
- May prevent lesions in the walls of arteries

Lecithin:

This is known as a phospholipid (type of fat) that is needed by all living cells. However, Lecithin **makes fats soluble** by binding fats & cholesterol to water, allowing your body to flush them out! A small amount is produced by our own bodies, but not enough to provide the multiple benefits it could. Lecithin can go hand in hand with Policosanol as a means of 'catching & releasing' the fats from the blood stream. 1200mg a day can provide the following:

- Emulsification of fats in the blood stream
- Has been proven to decrease cholesterol
- Promotes cardiovascular health
- Restores damaged livers
- Improve memory function in the brain
- May prevent gallstones & promote gallbladder health

Garlic:

This is a common herb and many people take it. However, not too many know the other uses for this supplement. The health benefits and medicinal properties of this natural herb have been long known. Taken in 600-900mg a day, benefits include:

- Managing high cholesterol levels
- Treat the symptoms of acne
- Can be used as a natural mosquito repellent
- Reduce inflammation in your body
- May prevent Cancer
- Fights infectious diseases
- Prevent weight gain
- Can help reduce high blood pressure

- ** if you take garlic as a supplement, you may notice that mosquitoes tend to leave you alone

Melatonin:

This is actually a naturally occurring hormone which your own body produces. 1-3mg is recommended for help in regulating and promoting sleep. Melatonin is often used for people suffering from insomnia. But sleep is not the only function of Melatonin; it also:

- Has strong Antioxidant properties
- Helps with Irregular Menstruation Cycles
- Maintains Cell Health
- Stimulates the production of Growth Hormone
- May help strengthen the Immune System

Black Pepper:

Interestingly enough, the human body only absorbs about 20-30% of most vitamins or nutrients you eat! So that Multi-Vitamin you have been taking every day is probably not doing as good a job as you think it has. Taken with Black Pepper or **Bioperine**, you can increase absorption to an additional 30-50%! It may be just a natural spice found in most every kitchen, but this simple staple has multiple other benefits:

- Enhances the absorption of nutrients
- Alleviates Hemorrhoids
- Alleviates Gas
- Alleviates Constipation
- Improves Digestion
- Stimulates the breakdown of fat cells
- Anti-bacterial & Anti-oxidant effect

COQ10:

Coenzyme Q10 is a compound that is made naturally in the body & actually found in every cell of your body! It is used by cells to produce energy needed for cell growth and maintenance; it is also used as an antioxidant. Antioxidants protect cells from chemical damage. A dosage of 30mg of COQ10 provides the following benefits:

- May protect damage to cells on a cellular level; even Cancer
- Has anti-aging properties
- Aids in circulation
- Increases oxygen in tissues
- Stimulates the immune system

- Aids tissues and cells to fight off infection
- Can help reduce high blood pressure
- Stimulates metabolism
- Plays a role in Heart Health

Your Heart & Liver contain the highest concentration of COQ10. Statins, such as Lipitor and Lovacol **inhibit the production of COQ10 in your body

Folic Acid:

Also referred to as Vitamin B9, this supplement has been the subject of growing scientific interest. While most studies have focused on heart health, some recent findings suggest that folic acid either has antidepressant properties or can act as an augmenting mediator for standard antidepressant treatment. Taken between 400 – 800ug's, its multiple benefits include:

- May protect against pregnancy birth defects
- A protective effect against cardiovascular diseases
- Protects against some types of cancer
- Protects against various neurological impairments
- Helps breakdown homocysteine in the blood
- Helps lower cholesterol

- May help lower high blood pressure

Green Tea:

The Chinese have known about the medicinal benefits of green tea since ancient times, using it to treat everything from headaches to depression. Tea has powerful antioxidants which protect cells and inhibits the growth of cancer cells. Although some of this may be inconclusive, the benefits listed here may be very real:

- Lowers cholesterol
- Treats infections
- Rheumatoid Arthritis
- Cardiovascular disease
- Impaired immune system
- Cancer inhibiting properties

As I have explained before, these supplements may or may not be beneficial to you, depending on your genetic makeup. Below you will find my **real Medical Charts** with statistics on how they have worked for me. My daily regimen was and still is: Folic Acid, Policosanol, COQ10, and Lecithin. I also had a cup of green tea each day.

I did not change my diet (which I should have done); nor did I have an exercise routine; and I was smoking a pack a day! As you can see, however, I managed to lower my total cholesterol from very high to close to normal in less than 2 years. I did this with no prescription or statin drugs, like my doctor wanted me to take. I did it through constant commitment to taking my supplements daily.

I strongly believe that if I had changed my diet from high-fat foods to a more manageable one, did some daily walking, and quit smoking; my results would have been outstanding! Luckily, at the finish of this book, I would have completed a few of those objectives.

Lipid Panel Results: 10/13/2006

CHOLESTEROL	167	<200- MG/DL
LDL		<100- MG/DL
	UNABLE TO CALCULATE DUE TO TRIGLYCERIDE >400. A DIRECT LDL HAS BEEN REFLEXIVELY ORDERED.	

HDL CHOLESTEROL	20	>39- MG/DL
TRIGLYCERIDE	609	<150- MG/DL

Lipid Panel Results: 01/17/2008

CHOLESTEROL	141	<200- MG/DL
LDL	110	<100- MG/DL
HDL CHOLESTEROL	32	>39- MG/DL
TRIGLYCERIDE	174	<150- MG/DL

****The following Herbs can also play a significant part in weight loss:**

Cayenne Pepper Capsules:

Cayenne's medicinal and culinary applications date back as far as 9,000 years, being used by Native Americans. Its benefits are derived from the capsaicin, which is the active ingredient. **Natural Weight Loss** is a by-product of this amazing herb.

A friend of mine, Rob, now lives by the benefits of this herb. Rob was a 375 pound man plagued with weight issues that led to sleep apnea, high blood pressure, and high cholesterol. He took one capsule with each meal (3 times a day) and combined with brisk walking, actually lost 85 pounds in 3 months!

When taking Cayenne, it is the **'Thermal Units'** (how hot it is) that counts, not how many you take. In Rob's case, he was using a supplement of 60,000 BTU's.

Benefits include:

- Weight Loss by tripling your metabolism
- Provides support for digestion
- Supports circulatory health
- May reduce the risk of heart attack
- May help boost energy & overcome fatigue
- Is a natural cure for stomach upset and ulcers (you wouldn't think that, would you?!)
- Reduce buildup of Sinus Pressure
- Useful in the treatment of Diarrhea

Cayenne has even been known to **stop Heart Attacks! This has worked by giving the victim the Cayenne in pure form, such as an Extract mixed in a hot liquid, like tea. It is one of the strongest natural stimulants known.

Psyllium Husk:

Interestingly enough, Psyllium Husk is actually the dietary fiber in Metamucil, an OTC fiber supplement. It comes from the crushed seeds of the Plantago Ovata plant and is primarily used for help with the digestive tract. 1,000 mg a day should do it. The benefits include:

- Colon cleansing
- Stabilizes blood pressure
- Heartburn remedy
- Lowers cholesterol
- Treatment for stomach and intestinal ulcers
- Constipation remedy
- May help with weight loss

Alpha-GPC:

This is a less talked about nutrient which is derived from Soy. This is known to some as an anti-aging supplement that has many related health benefits. 500-1200 milligrams per day can:

- Helps retain Memory
- Naturally releases Growth Hormone
- Protects Brain Cells from damage

- Improves Mood
- Reduces Body Fat
- Boosts Energy Levels
- Strengthens Immune System

Lemon Water:

Here's a smart bit of advice for everyone. Drink a glass of lukewarm water with a slice of lemon in it every single morning! It is simple, inexpensive, and readily available; lemons should always be room temperature. Lemons help alkalize your body, providing many benefits such as:

- Flushing out toxins from your body
- Stimulating the digestive system
- Helping with Urinary Tract Infections
- Relieving Nausea, Heartburn, & Bloating
- Acting as a Liver Tonic
- Curing Throat Infections
- Aiding in Dental Care & Toothaches
- Controlling High Blood Pressure
- Acting as a Blood Purifier

**LOSE THAT WEIGHT NATURALLY

Negative Calorie Foods:

There are certain foods available in your grocery store that will actually help you lose weight. These types of foods force your body to use more energy (calories) to digest them than the foods themselves provide.

As an example, a 5 calorie piece of celery can require 150 calories to digest, resulting in a net loss of 145 calories from total body fat! The more you eat vs. high-fats, the more weight you lose. Below you will find a small chart with a list of negative Calorie Foods:

NEGATIVE CALORIE VEGETABLES		
Spinach	Hot Chilies	Radish
Carrots	Cucumber	Lettuce
Cabbage	Turnips	Garden Cress
Beet Root	Chicory	Asparagus
Cauliflower	Green Beans	Onions
Celery	Garlic	Broccoli
Kale	Zucchini	Sauerkraut
Corn	Chives	Scallions

Artichokes	Leeks	Squash
Brussels Sprouts	Rutabagas	Pickles
Mushrooms	Endive	

NEGATIVE CALORIE FRUITS		
Peaches	Honeydew	Papaya
Pineapple	Grapefruit	Raspberries
Apples	Lemons	Strawberries
Blueberries	Limes	Tomatoes
Cranberry	Oranges	Tangerines
Cantaloupe	Mango	Watermelon
Pomegranate	Pears	Quince
Prunes	Kumquats	Damson Plums
Muskmelons	Loganberries	Currants
Apricots	Cherries	

NEGATIVE CALORIE PROTEINS		
Tuna	Lobster	Crab
Shrimp	Frog Legs	Trout
Sea Bass	Cod	Flounder
Oysters	Clams	Mussels
Abalone		

**Losing weight in any 'Extreme Way' can result in poor health & detrimental effects. You may include these foods in your diet, but please remember to eat sensibly.

NATURAL HERBS FOR:

Depression & Anxiety-

St. John's Wort has been shown to alleviate depression and anxiety; an added benefit is a gentle sedative effect.

Passionflower has a tranquilizing affect on the nervous system, thereby alleviating anxiety.

Ginko Biloba is a powerful anti-depressant and anti-oxidant that also increases blood flow to the brain.

Licorice contains some of the same inhibitors which are found in prescription medication for depression.

Type 2 Diabetes-

Cinnamon was found to improve blood glucose control in people suffering from Type 2 Diabetes.

Zinc seems to play an important part in the storage and production of insulin.

Garlic is a natural blood thinner and slows down production of free radicals and the process of glycation that occurs from high sugar levels.

Fenugreek seeds contain alkaloids that can increase the number of insulin receptors in red blood cells, while improving glucose utilization.

Hair Loss-

Honey with a paste of cinnamon and warm olive oil can be massaged into the scalp and left on for 30 minutes to promote hair growth.

Aloe Vera Gel has been used to promote healthy hair by healing the scalp, cleansing the pores, and balancing pH levels.

Rosemary (applied topically) is a centuries-old remedy for hair loss. It promotes new cell growth on the scalp as well as cleans and disinfects.

Saw Palmetto is one of the most popular natural treatments for baldness there is. It works well for a certain type of hair loss that affects the top of the head.

Stress Relief:

Whether your stress causes digestive problems, tension, or even anger, you can try these natural herbs: Chamomile, Peppermint, Valerian, Willow Bark, Ginseng, or even 250-500mg of Magnesium (the Anti-stress Mineral)!

Personal Thoughts:

So why is this information not readily available?! Two words: **Big Business**. What would a Mega-Pharmaceutical Corporation do as people begin to realize that an Herb grown in their backyards can essentially cure the same ailments as the OTC Product that they pay $3.99 for? In my opinion, they would stop it: using misdirection, scare tactics, and anything else to continue to dupe the Consumer into buying their products. Could this even be the reason that many Herbal Alternatives are not FDA approved?!

'These Statements Have Not Been Approved By the FDA'; does that sound pretty scary? To the average consumer, this simple statement is the deciding factor of purchasing an OTC medicine or taking the advice of a friend. Why is it that none of these amazing Herbs have been tested then? Wouldn't it make sense that since Herbs are so readily available that they would be the most logical choice to be screened for benefits to the general public?

My goal in this book is to simply make this information readily available and maybe save some lives and help people understand the un-tapped benefits of these herbal alternatives. I'll give you the information. Whether you use it or not, is up to you.

On a side note, I've told you about numerous Herbs that you can take with incredible results. However, no one seems to inform people **what not to take. It would simply be ridiculous to go through one after another because I will be here all day so I will stick to the most common issues where taking some Herbs will be a disadvantage rather than an advantage.

HERBS TO AVOID IF RECEIVING CHEMOTHERAPY:

Here is a list of some herbs **NOT TO** take if you are a Cancer patient who is in chemotherapy. These herbals can interfere with certain medicines:

- Garlic
- Ginseng
- Tumeric
- St. John's Wort
- Milk Thistle
- Goldenseal
- Ginkgo
- Dong Quai
- Shitake Mushroom
- Chrysanthemum

HERBS TO AVOID WHEN PREGNANT:

- Natural Laxatives
- Uterine Stimulants
- Alkaloids, Licorice, Thyme, Passion Flower, Rhubarb
- Essential Oils such as Lavender, Fennel, Rosemary, Sage, Thyme, Juniper, Cayenne, or Marjoram

CHAPTER 2

NATURAL USES FOR EVERYDAY PRODUCTS:

Lemon Juice:

-disinfect your home with lemon juice: lemon juice's acidic content is so strong that it can kill bacteria

-rinse your hair with it to give hair a silky shine

-heal & soothe a sore throat by swallowing a mixture of lemon and honey

-dab some on a cut or scrape to disinfect it

-cure dandruff by applying it to your hair; repeat this for a week or so

-relieve poison ivy itch

-use it to neutralize fridge smells by cutting one in half and keeping in your fridge

-apply equal parts water and lemon juice for a natural air freshener

Coca-Cola:

-dabbed on aluminum foil removes rust; yep – same stuff we drink on a regular basis

-can loosen rusty bolts

-kills slugs and snails; put some in a small bowl and leave it by the infestation

-cleans burnt pots and pans; let it soak and then rinse away

-cleans car battery terminals

-removes gum from hair

-clean your toilet bowl

Vinegar:

-add a little to your pet's drinking water; it can control fleas, helps with arthritic conditions, and puts a shine to their coats

-deter ants by spraying along trails

-eliminate animal urine stains from carpets by blotting with equal parts vinegar and cool water

-kill weeds in your garden by spraying full strength

-kills unwanted grass in cracks or sidewalks

-polish chrome wheels on your car

-apply equal parts vinegar and glycerin to remove warts

-rub on to remove tough stains

-make brass, copper, and pewter shine

-remove hard water stains; put on a cloth and drape

-make no-wax linoleum shine

Baking Soda:

-use it as a face and body scrub

-relieves itch from insect bites

-relieve your baby's diaper rash; put 3 tablespoons in the bath water

-apply on a jellyfish sting to draw out the venom

-reduce cigarette odor; sprinkle it on ashtrays

-repel cockroaches, ants, and other insects

-absorbs odor from kitty litter

-add a teaspoon to your dishwasher to clean better]

-use it as a household cleaner

-clean and absorb odors from trash cans

-clean your barbecue grill

-is a non-toxic teeth whitener

-bake a cake – haha!

Petroleum Jelly:

-moisturize rough feet

-safely removes make-up

-as a lip gloss

-prevent razor burn

-prevent diaper rash

-remove a stuck ring from your finger

-remove lipstick stains

-remove gum from wood

-restore shine to leather

-soothe a pet's sore paws

Bounce:

-Repel Mosquitoes by tying a sheet to your self

-Dissolve soap scum from shower doors

-Eliminate static cling from pantyhose

-Collect Pet Hair

CHAPTER 3

Okay, this section I put in here because my Wife was complaining that this book is not just for the Guys. Don't know what she means by that, but here goes-

HOW TO INDUCE LABOR NATURALLY:

- Herbal supplements such as Evening Primrose Oil or Chamomile to soften your Cervix (ask your doctor about dosage)
- Eat Pineapple or Spicy Foods
- March up and down Stairs
- Have Sex to release Oxytocin (causes uterus to contract)
- Nipple Stimulation to release Oxytocin (causes uterus to contract)
- Squatting
- Get a Massage to relieve Tension

WHAT SHOULD I PACK FOR THE HOSPITAL (when having a baby):

- Health Insurance Card

- Photo I.D.
- Slippers
- Socks
- Comfortable clothing such as sweatpants
- Hair Tie
- Camera
- Lotion
- Toothbrush
- Change for Vending
- Baby Car Seat
- Cell Phone
- Baby Clothing, Diapers, & Warm Jacket
- Notepad & Pen
- Sanitary Pads

HOW TO NATURALLY INCREASE YOUR CHANCES OF FERTILITY AND HAVING A BABY

(Yes, this one's for women only but the men are more than welcome to give it a shot)**:**

Take these Vitamins:

Vitamin C and Antioxidants – these vitamins will boost sperm quality and prevent certain sperm defects

Calcium and Vitamin D – these vitamins will strengthen your bones and your babies; it will also prepare your body for pregnancy. Vitamin D will also allow your body to absorb calcium at triple the rate of normal.

Zinc – is one of the most widely studied nutrient in for increasing fertility; it is an essential component of genetic material and is necessary to efficiently utilize reproductive hormones

Selenium – is an antioxidant that helps to protect your body from free radicals and also maximizes sperm formation

Vitamin E – studies have shown that the antioxidant activity of this vitamin makes sperm more fertile

Try these Herbs:

Vitex/Chaste Tree Berry – this herb will restore hormonal imbalances in your body, thereby increasing the chances of fertility

Evening Primrose Oil – helps alleviate PMS (**Yay**!) and aids in the production of cervical fluid

Ginseng – not for you, but have your hubby take it; it stimulates the immune system and improves male fertility while fighting male impotence

Try this OTC method:

Progesterone Cream – the one most essential hormone for conception and important for the survival of a fertilized egg and fetus through gestation; it can also be prescribed

**These treatments must be carefully recommended by your doctor. Please make sure you inform your physician on everything you are taking as some complications may occur if herbs or vitamins are used in the wrong combination.

Nature's Viagra:

No one likes to utter the words 'Erectile Disfunction'. At least I don't, but for those are familiar with it, try 100mg of Ginkgo Biloba or 1gram of L-Arginine 3 times a day! They are not guaranteed, but with a 50/50 success rate, it can't hurt!

The following was written to help with the common nightmare of **MOVING!** There have been many times where I have moved from one city or state to another, only to regret my decision. There is actually a whole lot more to moving than I previously thought so I'm putting this section in here. Good Luck!

ARE YOU PLANNING ON MOVING? No matter where you are going, the main thing you should do is some research on what lies there for you and your family. Here are some criteria to concentrate on and even some interesting facts on different States:

Criteria for Moving-

- What is the Job Market?
- What is the Median Home Pricing?
- How much can you get the Same Home for in Both Areas?
- What are the Property Taxes and Insurance Rates?
- What are the Utility Costs?
- What are the Medical Costs?
- Is there a Hospital close by?
- What is the trend of Economy?
- Is there a good Education System and Good Schools? (www.greatschools.net)
- What is the Quality of Life?
- Is there Diversity & Culture?
- What are the Good Neighborhoods?

- How is the Traffic?
- How long does it take to get from the Outskirts to the Downtown Area?
- What are the Crime Statistics?
- What is the Cost of Living?
- What is the Weather like?
- What Family Events & Activities are in the area?
- What are the Daycare Costs?
- Does your Cell Phone Carrier have towers there?

States that DO NOT have (State) Income Tax-

- Alaska
- Florida
- Nevada
- South Dakota
- Texas
- Washington
- Wyoming

States that do not require Auto Insurance-

- Wisconsin
- New Hampshire

States that DO NOT have (State) Income Tax-

- Alaska
- Delaware
- Montana
- New Hampshire
- Oregon

**Do a check in your preferred Neighborhood for Sexual Predators: http://www.familywatchdog.us/

5 TOP PAYING JOBS:

- Anesthesiologists /Anesthetic Nurse
- Physician
- Psychiatrist
- Sales Director
- Actuary

CHAPTER 4

THINGS YOU MAY WANT TO KNOW:

How to handle an IRS Audit: There are common mistakes that most people will make because they assume that giving an Auditor everything is required. According to the law, you only need to provide an IRS Auditor with the documentation (taxes, paperwork, etc.) that the deduction is being questioned on. Never give them more or less information that is required **e.g.** previous year's taxes.

Here are some reasons why you may be audited:

- Profit Margin is much lower than normal
- High Travel & Entertainment
- Little to No Profit
- Higher than usual Auto Expenses
- Higher than usual Mileage

How to Tell If Someone Is Lying: Here are some clues that FBI personnel are trained to notice that someone is lying, nervous, or trying to hide something.

- Turning their eyes up and to the right while speaking

- Fidgeting, rapid blinking, tapping, itching, scratching
- Touching their face, biting their nails, or covering their mouth
- Raising their voice to a high level
- Pausing for unusually long periods
- Exaggerated story-telling or drawn out story
- No eye contact or looking away when speaking

Health Concerns with Plastics:

Have you ever noticed that there are numbers enclosed in a triangle of arrows imprinted on most plastics? Most people do not know what they mean, but believe me when I tell you that some of these plastics have the potential to negatively affect your health and the health of your child!

Phthalates, the technical term for this dangerous class of industrial compounds is used in the softening of plastics, in some perfumes, hairsprays, lubricants, baby bottles, pacifiers, rattles, toys, and so many more household products that it would make quite a list.

**Please remember that Phthalates are not found in everything listed above; some products are manufactured with no Phthalates whatsoever. Do not start throwing out every plastic you own.

Phthalates have been linked to human toxicology, cancers, infertility, improper fetal development, endocrine disruption, low sperm count, and many other health concerns.

For now, we are focusing on Plastics and what the numbers mean. **These numbers do two things: they tell you which plastics are safe and which ones are not & can be recycled.** Plastics with numbers **1, 2, 4, & 5 are generally considered safe**. Plastics with numbers **3, 6, & 7 are the ones to watch out for!**

How to Stop a Kitchen Oil Fire: This is a must-know for everyone and everyone who thinks they already know how. If a pan of oil catches fire, follow these steps:

1. Turn off the heat

2. Run a washcloth under cold water

3. Wring the water out of the washcloth

4. Cover the pan completely and wait until it has cooled down

Beware of ASBESTOS:

I think this is so important because it happened to me: my first home I purchased was an older one with an Asbestos floor. Asbestos is a mineral fiber that was commonly used for insulation & a fire retardant. Stay away from Asbestos! If you are buying a home or commercial building, make sure you get an inspection done and refuse it on the spot if it contains any amount of Asbestos!

Asbestos fibers can be inhaled into the lungs, where they can cause significant health issues! It takes 39 Years to clear the air of asbestos in an indoor facility once you remove it. Beware – you will have many more problems attributed to it down the line as well.

How to avoid Hip Replacement or Hip Problems:

There are a few easy ways to do this: **1** – most of us carry our wallets in our back pockets. Unfortunately, this is the worst way to carry it and can cause hip and back problems in the near future.

Each time you sit down, your hips misalign and stay that way until you get back up. Hold your wallet or money clip in your **front pocket** instead to keep your hips from getting misaligned. It is a very easy change to make and can greatly reduce costly medical bills!

2-When running or active, make sure you warm up first and concentrate on your form.

DETOX:

Your Body goes through so much 'wear & tear' over the years that we have to give it a **'Tune-up'** every so often to maintain our systems and remain healthy. I'm sure you've all heard the phrase, **'You may not remember the first hot dog you ate, but your body does'**. What that means is there are always remnants of foods & waste that in time, turn into **toxins**. Most of you know of 'Colon Cleansing' and other Body Detoxification Procedures, but are unsure of which ones work and which ones are some useless fad.

In the following few pages, I'm going to give you some **detailed steps to fine-tune and cleanse your body's vital organs**. These are the 'powerhouses' that 'keep the machine running'.

How to Detox your Kidneys:

1) Buy some Parsley – yes, you heard right – Parsley

2) Wash it and chop it up into small pieces

3) Boil it (10 minutes) in a pot of clean water
4) Put it in the fridge to cool down
5) Filter the water and pour it into a clean container
6) Drink 1 8oz glass in the morning and 1 8oz glass in the evening

How to Detox your Liver:

** A 'Kindey Cleanse' is highly recommended before the Liver Detox

First, you must get rid of any parasites (yes, I said Parasites) by following these steps and using these herbal ingredients:

- Wormwood Capsules (300mg)
- Black Walnut Hull Tincture Extra Strength (Drops)
- Clove Capsules (500mg)
- Ornithine –Amino Acid(500mg)

- **Black Walnut** – 6 day treatment: Take 1 drop in accordance with the day you are on. For example – Day 1, take 1 drop in a ½ cup glass of water, Day 2, take 2 drops and so on until you reach Day 6. On this day, take 2 teaspoons in ¼ cup of water. SIP; don't GULP! Take 2 teaspoons once the second week.

- **Clove Capsules** – Day 1 take 1 capsule 3 times before meals. Day 2 take 2 capsules 3 times a day, Days 3-10 take 3 capsules 3 times a day. After Day 10, you can take 3 capsules once a week.

- **Wormwood Capsules** – Days 1 & 2 take 1 capsule before supper, Days 3 & 4 take 2 capsules before supper. Increase the capsules by 1 every 2 Days. After the treatment, you can take 7 capsules once a week.
- Take 4 **Ornithine** to help you sleep!

Now, you can continue with your Liver Detoxification

1) Fast for 2-3 days by drinking water and fruit juices; if you are very hungry, try eating fruits and vegetables. Do not cook them as we are trying to keep everything natural.

2) You will need: 4 Tablespoons of Epsom Salts, 3 cups of Water, ½ cup of Olive Oil (left out in open), freshly squeezed Grapefruit Juice, 10-20 drops of Black Walnut Tincture, and 4-8 Ornithine tablets.

3) Choose a 2-day interval for the cleanse and remember to not take any medicines, vitamins, or any other supplement that day. Eat a no-fat breakfast such as bread and jam, but no dairy.

4) Do not eat or drink after 2:00 PM. Mix 4 tablespoons of the Epsom Salts in 3 cups water (better tasting when ice cold).

5) 6:00PM - Drink a ¾ cup of the mixture and if you need, a few mouthfuls of water.

6) 8:00PM – Drink a ¾ cup of the mixture.

7) 9:45PM – Pour ½ cup olive oil into a **separate container**. Wash the grapefruit in hot water and dry, squeezing by hand into a measuring cup. After you have at least ½ to ¾ cup, add it to the olive oil and also add 10-20 drops of Black Walnut Tincture. Shake hard until watery.

8) **Visit the bathroom

9) 10:00PM – Drink the mixture and take 4 Ornithine capsules. Use a straw to make it go down easier and Honey as a chaser. Lie down immediately and fall asleep, trying hard to keep perfectly still for at least 20 minutes.

10) Morning – Wake up and take your third dose of Epsom Salt mixture; after 6:00AM!

11) 2 HOURS LATER take your fourth dose of the Epsom Salt mixture and go back to bed if you'd like or lay down.

12) AFTER 2 MORE HOURS, you may eat. Start yourself slowly with fruit juice and then solid fruits slowly throughout the day.

You will pass many **gallstones (without much pain thanks to the Epsom Salts) throughout the procedure, but the **toxicity and**

most liver issues will be much less than before, if not gone altogether. You can repeat the treatments every two weeks for further improvement!

How to Treat a Bee Sting:

- Run away from the Bee! (Seriously)
- Remove the Stinger using a tweezers or your fingers.
- Check to see if you or the person you are helping is having an allergic reaction; including itching, redness, hives, or shortness of breath (If this is the case, call 911). It is common for non-allergic victims to have some of these reactions; however, shortness of breath or difficulty in swallowing is not.
- Put a cool, wet compress on the inflamed area.
- Apply some calamine lotion to the sting and take some acetaminophen.

Natural Ways to Cure/Lessen Acne:

- Lemon Juice – using a cotton ball, swab some on your face before bedtime
- Aloe Vera Gel – has anti-inflammatory & anti-bacterial properties to clear up your skin

- Tea Tree Oil – smells awful, but is a very effective acne fighter (only use externally)
- Anything to relieve Stress

Top Cancer-causing Foods:

- Hot Dogs – very high in cancer-causing nitrates
- Processed Meats – very high in cancer-causing nitrates
- Bacon – high in saturated fats
- Doughnuts – high in concentrated white flour, sugar, and hydrogenated oils
- French Fries – high in hydrogenated oils and contain acryl amides when fried
- Packaged Cookies, Chips, & Crackers – high in concentrated white flour and sugar

Save your own life if you are having a Heart Attack: A person usually has about 10 seconds after the onset of a Heart Attack before they lose consciousness. To keep yourself alive, remember these steps:

1. Try your damndest not to panic – I know – easier said than done, right?

2. Take a deep breath and force yourself to cough deep and with vigor

3. Repeat this process every 2 seconds

4. Keep doing it until help arrives or your heart regains a normal rhythm

The deep breaths and deep coughing will force your lungs to keep oxygen flowing through your body and keep your blood circulating. The coughing also causes the squeezing pressure on the heart, helping it to beat normally. Pass this information along to everyone you can; it may save a life!

Get rid of Warts with Duct Tape:

What?! No, you heard me right. The most common ways for a doctor to remove a Wart is through 'Freezing' or in 'at home' using a treatment with salicylic acid.

Instead, try this:

1. Simply place a piece of Duct Tape over a Wart and keep it dry.

2. After a shower or swim, remove the tape and soak the Wart.

3. Try to rub off the dead skin on top using an emery board or stone and let it dry.

4. After 24 hours, place a new piece of Duct Tape over the Wart.

5. Repeat this process for about 4-6 weeks or until the Wart drops off.

Immune System Boosters: Need something to help you fight those Viruses/Bacterium during the Flu Season, besides Vitamin C? Try some of these:

- Vitamin D (Thanks Dr. Lang)
- Beta-carotene – usually found in any brightly colored vegetable
- Zinc
- Garlic
- B Vitamins
- Acidophilus or other Probiotic Supplement
- Protein – from lean meats
- Green Tea

Why You Should Avoid Chemical Sweeteners:

Artificial Sugars have been around for a very long time and used in everything from diet sodas to alternative sugar packets. Here's some information on them you may not have known:

Saccharin – the most commonly used form of artificial sweeteners has been linked to cancer in animals and allergic reactions in humans.

Sucralose – research has shown that this chemical has shown abnormalities in the thymus gland, liver, and kidneys.

Tagatose – tests have found that patients who have consumed large amounts of this have experienced digestive tract irritation and nausea.

Stevia – naturally comes from the leaves of the Stevia plant, but has been linked to concerns of blood sugar control and infertility.

Aspartame – headaches have been shown to be the most common side effect, but reports of panic attacks, hallucinations, and depression have been reported.

I'm not going to tell you to look negatively on every artificial sweetener known to man, because many things have side effects. I am simply telling you that these are man-made substances that are not natural. Follow your own discretion with them.

How you can tell the difference between North, South, East, & West:

Have you ever met those people who can just automatically know which direction they are speaking of without a compass? Here are some tips to help you know this as well:

- ➢ Remember that both the Sun and the Moon rise in the East and set in the West
- ➢ West is to the left, East is to the right
- ➢ Roads, avenues, lanes, and places usually run East and West
- ➢ Streets, terraces, and drives usually run North and South
- ➢ A Compass will point to Magnetic North; not True North

Stay Warm During the Winter:

Why am I putting this in here? Believe me when I say there are a few tricks most people still do not know.

- ✓ Make sure gloves or mittens have 'wiggle room'. If they are too tight or too small, they can prevent proper blood circulation. If this happens, it does not matter how dry your gloves are – your hands will freeze!
- ✓ Drink an 8 oz glass of water every hour or few hours, depending how cold it is outside. Your body needs water to keep your blood circulating to warm it.
- ✓ **Avoid** wearing **COTTON** Thermal Underwear! It is useless as cotton soaks in water and saturates your skin with water. Once it freezes, you get colder. Use a Synthetic, like Polyester or Polypropylene, which wicks water away from your skin!

CHAPTER 5

DID YOU KNOW

- In some Hospitals, the length of the 'white coat' is directly related to the amount of training a Doctor has had; the longer the better?

-By slowly raising your legs and lying on your back, that you cannot sink in Quicksand?

-It is impossible to lick your elbow?

-Honey is the only food that cannot spoil?

-Not one word in the English language rhymes with Orange, Month, or Purple?

-That you can use ½ of the recommended amount of Laundry Detergent and still get your dirty clothes just as clean? Companies just tell you to use the 'standard' measurement as a gimmick to sell more detergent.

-20% of the world's population lives in China?

-The most spoken language in the world is Mandarin?

-That you can sharpen Scissors or Knives using Aluminum Foil, Sandpaper, or even Steel Wool?

-You burn more calories sleeping than watching TV?

-The place that has the most germs in your car is your dashboard?

-Most office desks have hundreds of times more bacteria than your average toilet?

-Fingernails grow 4 times faster than toe nails?

-Most lipstick contains fish scales?

-The FDA allows 1 rat hair per 100 grams of chocolate and no more than 60 insect fragments per 100 grams?

-Many people still have bad breath and leftover bacteria after brushing simply because they do not brush their tongues?

-Some of your brain cells die every time you sneeze?

-The sound you hear from a seashell is actually the blood rushing through your ears?

-There are no clocks in Las Vegas Casinos?

-Half an ounce of gas is used to start the average car?

-Human teeth are close to the hardness of rocks?

-Human thigh bones are stronger than concrete?

-The State of Florida is larger than England?

-The opposite sides of a cubed Dice always add up to 7?

-Eating an apple in the morning is better than caffeine?

-You can only see a Rainbow if your back is to the sun?

-Peanuts are used in the production of dynamite?

-The average person falls asleep in 7 minutes?

-The Declaration of Independence was written on hemp?

-Most mosquito repellents work by hiding the human scent, not by repelling mosquitoes?

-A square piece of paper cannot be folded in halves more than 7 times?

-Most dust particles are made from human skin?

-An average human eats 8 spiders while asleep in their lifetime?

-Your strongest muscle in your body is your Tongue?

-You can usually negotiate the price of a mattress in most (Furniture) stores; sometimes mattresses are marked up as much as 500%. Ask for the discount, but ask discreetly.

-That Gum Disease can increase the risk of heart attack by 200-400%? Brush your TONGUE, not just your Teeth!

-Citronella Candles may contain Paraffin Wax, which can cause respiratory disease? Make sure the candles are made with only Soy Wax. Soy Wax is also a very effective bug repellent.

-You can entertain your kids educationally at www.noggin.com

-Rubbing Vitamin E Oil into a scar can help it heal?

-You can save your lawn from Brown Patches from pet urine by spreading lime or gypsum across your yard?

-You can find, research, and diagnose your Medical Problems & Conditions online in one easy-to-read database: http://www.nlm.nih.gov/medlineplus/?

-Most of what you hear and believe in the Media is only what ***they*** want you to hear and believe? Trust me – it's been happening for centuries. I'm not a 'conspiracy theorist', but seriously- look at the state of things today and how they've gotten that way. Take a look at: www.morningson.info and find out exactly who the Illuminati are…

CHAPTER 6

THE LEADING CAUSES OF DEATH IN THE U.S.

#1 - Heart Disease

#2 – Cancer

#3 – Stroke

#4 – Chronic lower respiratory diseases

#5 – Accidents

#6 – Diabetes

#7 – Alzheimer’s disease

#8 – Influenza & Pneumonia

#9 – Nephritis, Nephrotic Syndrome

#10 – Septicemia

The biggest 2 changes we can make that do not cost us anything extra are Diet & Exercise. I know – it’s easier said than done. What is it that makes it so difficult to do something so easy?

I believe it is a combination of lack of willpower, easy access, and taking things for granted. If you have one of the above diseases, then look for herbal alternatives to help deal with symptoms and problems associated with that particular disease.

Natural Ways to Stop Smoking:

I still remember how difficult it was to stop smoking. The very first time was due to my Father's insistence that my brother and I quit right on the spot. He threw his cigarettes in the trash and we followed suit. The next morning, all three of us met at the trash can to help each other dig the cigarettes out! Lucky for you – these herbs may help:

Ginseng – This herb has been shown to prevent the nicotine-induced release of dopamine. Dopamine is what makes people feel good after a cigarette.

Lobelia – This is a controversial herbal remedy that acts as a physical relaxant and nerve depressant. It elevates the levels of dopamine in the brain that is similar to nicotine.

St. Johns Wort – As Zyban was accidentally found to help people stop smoking, so too has St. Johns Wort. It also elevates the dopamine levels in the brain as well as helping with the depression caused by withdrawal.

Want to know how to save big $$$ on everything??

Check out www.StealDeals.net and www.Techbargains.com . Consumers like yourself will post the next best deal that they find so you don't have to do all the work!

Extended Warranties: Most stores make more money off these than any other product they sell! There will almost always be at least a one-year Manufacturer's Warranty on most electronics you purchase and most times, this is all you will need. If something is to happen that is hardware or software related it will assuredly occur within the first year. Even though these plans typically run you between 10 and 30% of the product purchase price, most times, they do not cover any accidental damage! If the warrant is cost-effective with good coverage, I'd suggest purchasing it.

Credit Card Secrets: Don't they make enough money already without having to hold back important information from us? Yep. Here are a few things you may not have known:

- Some Premium Cards have perks that automatically extend the warranty on your purchase
- Most Credit Agencies are extremely flexible – if your interest rate is too high or you were charged a late fee, give them a call and ask them to do something about it. If they decline, let them know that you will be going with someone else. Trust me – most times they will budge
- Some Credit Cards do not have a foreign transaction fee charge
- Most Credit Cards offer auto rental liability insurance, effectively covering loss and collision

- After the first year or two, you may be able to request an increase to your credit limit without them doing a credit check

- Do not co-sign for your child's credit card; have them co-sign a card that you get instead. This way, you can keep track of spending and know where your money is going. You can then cancel the card if limits are breached and your son or daughter will still build their credit.

- Raise your Credit Rating the easy way! Have a friend or family member with a high credit rating add your name to his or her card as an accepted user. Each time they make a purchase and pay it off, your credit will rise as well!

The Benefits of a Roth IRA:

- Earnings will continue to grow Tax-Free

- Most anyone who earns income can open one

- All withdrawals are Tax-Free! (After age 59 ½, and if the account has been in existence for at least 5 years) Up to $10,000 in earnings withdrawals are considered tax-free if the money is used to purchase a main residence for a 1st time home buyer (some rules apply)

- If the owner of a Roth IRA dies, the spouse becomes the beneficiary
- Assets can be passed on to heirs
- The best way to improve your memory is to clean your desk; it forces your brain to be both creative & logical

WHEN IS THE BEST TIME TO BUY:

If you are like me, then you will want to know how to save the most money on the things we all need and the best time to buy. You can save a ton of money simply by purchasing products to coincide with the time of season, month of the year, or even the day of the week that the manufacturer offers substantial savings.

Airline Tickets – Tuesday nights between 11pm and 1am are the times that Airlines make most of their major pricing changes. It also helps to fly out on and return on any weekday, but Friday; mid-week is preferable. For some airlines, you will get better fares if you fly out on a Saturday and return on a Tuesday.

Another way you might consider is to buy your tickets from a Consolidator. They purchase these tickets at a bulk discount or wholesale.

New Car or Truck – At the end of each month (second to last day is best), Dealers & Salesman who need to fill their monthly quota will usually discount the car to you. At the end of the Model Year, the last year's model miraculously begins to lose its high prices and discounts galore start to show up. At the end of September, October, and November are also prime times to purchase a new vehicle because most new models have started to arrive; these are also winter months. Special promotions, rebates, and money-saving discounts also coincide with 3-day holiday weekends.

Gadgets & Electronics – Most electronics manufacturers release their new models in the Spring so many of the 'older' models will see significant price slashing during the months of late March, April, and May. Better yet, electronics seem to be severely discounted during Black Friday (Day after Thanksgiving-duh) or now that these big corporations want to get even more of your money, they created Cyber Monday in 2005.

Furniture – This one has some complications because of the 'different types' of furniture. For example, 'Office Furniture' is discounted at the usual beginning of a fiscal year – January. 'Dining Room Furniture' is discounted during the Holiday Season – October, November, & December. 'Living Room Furniture' is the same. Bedroom Sets can be purchased for a great price during any 3-day holiday weekend sales or during major holidays. Obviously, 'Patio Furniture' can see some severe discounts right a month after summer officially ends.

New Bike – Most of the new models come out in the early part of the year. The best times to buy are January, February, and March.

New Snow Blower – Manufacturer's usually begin production in the late spring through summer months. The best deals are found at the end of the winter season, but don't wait too long because most retailers do not keep them in stock; otherwise, right around August is fine.

New Home – Of course, this is the most important investment most people will ever make so it is vital that you heed my advice. Springtime (Late March, April, & May) is the best time for great deals on a home! I'll mention the obvious for those critics. If you factor in the state of the economy (recession), the trend in the housing market, natural disasters, and interest rates – then the best time to buy a home is sadly, when times are tough.

The very best thing you can do **before you make an offer is to go onto the local County Treasurer's Land Records Search and do some research as to what the home is actually worth! You can also find out if the Seller has any delinquent taxes, what the land and improvements are worth, whom the Property Owner is, and so much more. Using this information, you can make the best offer that will mutually benefit both buyer and seller. Then again, in real estate - timing is everything!

The Truth About the Car Dealerships:

Purchasing a new vehicle is the second biggest decision you will usually make, besides of course, your first home. Everyone is naturally wary of new car salesman because we all feel that we may get 'taken for a ride'. We have come to believe that most of them are dishonest, greedy, even fake. Some of them are just that and you will get scammed if you do not know how the game works.

In some new car dealerships, commissions are based on the 'payable gross' to the dealership and applied in tiers. For example, if the payable gross was from $0 to $749, the commission paid would be 20 percent of the profit; $750 to $1249, it would be 25 percent and above $1250, would be 30 percent in commissions. Obviously, the motivated salespeople try to get the highest percentile bracket.

The Scam: On the customer deal worksheet, the car information is written along the top and the sticker price of the car in large numbers to stress the price of the car. **'Plus Fees'** is always written nest to the car price. The worksheet will soon become a mess of numbers.

The process begins by asking the customer how much they want to a monthly payment. Usually they say an even number, such as

$300. The salesman will counter that number by saying, '…up to?. Once the customer is baited and they say a larger figure, such as up to $350, guess which monthly payment they are going to get? This same 'trick' may be done with the down payment too.

The last box is for a trade-in. The dealership is aware because buyers are so eager to get into their new car, they often overlook the true value of the trade-in. A lower price that what the car is usually worth is almost always marked. This completes the worksheet in 4 Headers:

- Purchase Price of the Car
- Trade-in
- Down payment
- Monthly Payment

This allows the salesman to sell a car in different ways. For example, if the customer was determined to get full value for this trade-in, you could take extra profit from the purchase price or the financing.

The salesperson will offer the customer a drink or something to relax them, before making a call to the front to ask if this vehicle is still available. This creates urgency. Next, he will give you the highest price. In fact, these numbers are intentionally based on very high interest rates that are calculated on 5 year loans.

Obviously, the customer is angry about the $600 a month payment vs. the $300 one he agreed to. Now it's the salesperson's turn to be the 'good guy' by crossing out the high numbers and putting in lower ones. This, of course, builds a sense of trust between customer and salesman. A point to be taken is that they will never use even numbers so that it looks legitimate. Sooner or later, the number will add up to the 'up to price' of $350 a month.

Next, the salesperson will work on the trade-in. They will call the used car manager and ask what prices the dealership paid out for similar cars. The offers will come back at ridiculously low numbers. A customer expecting to get $6000 for their trade-in is now very easy to settle for $3000. Front-end money is made on the commissions and back-end money was made on the interest, holdbacks, and other parts of the deal.

A **Holdback** is a payment/commission that the manufacturer pays the dealer for selling the car; sometimes up to $1000 as well as additional manufacturer discounts and incentives. It is wise to remember that most cars on the lot that have been there over 90 days will earn no holdback for the dealer. After 90 days, the dealership has to dip into its own profits to keep the car on the lot. On special orders, the dealer makes a pure profit on the car, as they do not have floor plan financing. With these cars, you can wheel and deal to get a great price.

**A TIP to help you get through it:

Never negotiate on **Monthly Payment;** simply on the **purchase price of the vehicle!!**

TIPS and HINTS (to getting your vehicle for the best price):

- Automakers typically introduce new-model-year cars in August or September; a 2008 new car will be cheaper than a 2009, however – you have already lost a year in resale value
- Buy when a car is going to be re-designed; the older versions will be less expensive
- Buy at the end of the Month when sales quotas need to be met (the last week)
- Rebates often coincide with a holiday, long weekend, or special promotion
- Try not to act like you're a kid in a candy store; play it calm so the salesman does not know he has an 'easy sale'
- Come to the Dealership with several other Dealer Quotes (you can obtain these online)
- Some Credit Unions/Banks have a designated person to help you get a new vehicle for a great price; use them

CHAPTER 7

MORTGAGE TIPS & TRICKS: (What the Bank Doesn't Want You To Know)

DID YOU KNOW...

1) The Bank will hold your money until the 15th even though your mortgage payment is due on the 1st? What does this do?

   The Bank will hold the money so that they can get the most return on their investment; therefore, while your money is making dividends overnight, on holidays, and any other time you do not see it, you are being billed an additional 15 days of Interest you otherwise would not have had!

2) When you **Refinance**, your Interest Payments actually start all over again!!

   How? A large chunk of your Mortgage Payment is Interest. For example, when you start your payments, the Interest to Principal payment is 80-20. Each month that your loan is active, the Bank will graciously add an additional dollar or so to your principal payment. This gradually brings your interest down and your principal higher.

Let's say you have finally paid your Mortgage down to where the Interest to Principal payment is now 50-50. When you Refinance, it is essentially a 'new loan' so the payments are lower, but the Interest starts all over again! You are now back to an Interest to Principal payment of 80-20!

3) Before you even start looking for a home, get pre-approved and hire a home inspector. Getting pre-approved will save you a lot of time from looking at homes that you cannot afford and allow you to make a serious offer. Try to hire a home inspector who has some mechanical background; he or she could save you thousands by pointing out hidden problems and defects.

4) When is the halfway point of your Home Pay-off on a 30 year loan?
   It's not 15 years; it's actually 21 years!

HOW MUCH ARE YOU REALLY PAYING A MONTH IN MORTGAGE INTEREST?

Now, I realize this question belongs in the 'Mortgage Section', but trust me – I will show you why it deserves its own heading. This answer will shock you just like it did me when someone showed me the numbers. We will need an example, so I will use the following home with no down payment:

Mortgage: $100,000

Mortgage Term: 360 months or 30 years

Interest Rate: 6%

Mortgage Start Date: January 1st, 2010

As you can see, we have just purchased a new home for $100,000 on a 30-year fixed loan at 6% Interest. How much interest are we paying? The loan states 6%, right? We could not be more wrong!

An Amortization Calculator will show how much Interest we are paying throughout the life of our loan. Let's take the 1st year:

****Use this calculation:** PMT, CPT, IY = Actual Interest Paid / Calculations are in ( )

START OF LOAN: 1st YEAR

Monthly Payment: $599.55 (Principal + Interest)

Month	Payment	Principal	Interest	Total Interest	Balance Owed

Jan. 2010	$599.55	$99.55	$500.00	$500.00	$99,900.45
Feb. 2010	$599.55	$100.05	$499.50	$999.50	$99,800.40
Mar. 2010	$599.55	$100.55	$499.00	$1,498.50	$99,699.85
April 2010	$599.55	$101.05	$498.50	$1,997.00	$99,598.80
May 2010	$599.55	$101.56	$497.99	$2,495.00	$99,497.24
June 2010	$599.55	$102.06	$497.49	$2,992.48	$99,395.18
July 201	$599.55	$102.57	$496.98	$3,489.46	$99,292.61

0					
Aug. 2010	$599.55	$103.09	$496.46	$3,985.92	$99,189.52
Sept. 2010	$599.55	$103.60	$495.95	$4,481.87	$99,085.92
Oct. 2010	$599.55	$104.12	$495.43	$4,977.30	$98,981.79
Nov. 2010	$599.55	$104.64	$494.91	$5,472.21	$98,877.15
Dec. 2010	$599.55	$105.16	$494.39	$5,966.59	$98,771.99

END OF LOAN: 1st YEAR

Equity: $1228 (PV) – Equity built in a given year

12 Months: (N) – Number of years

Payment: (P+I) – Enter as a negative number / e.g. -$599.55

(PMT, CPT, IY =)

What percentage of **Interest** am I actually paying for my first year on my loan? Not 6%; actually
568.69%!!

HOW DO I PRE-QUALIFY FOR A LOAN?

Banks don't lend money to just anybody. There are certain conditions you must meet in order for a Bank to feel secure that you will pay them back. Whether it be for a home loan, a personal loan, or even an auto loan, most guidelines must be met. Here is what they are looking for:

- Some kind of Down Payment (usually between 3-20%)
- How good is your Credit (order a credit report yourself for free once a year)
- What is your Monthly Income (usually a lender looks for 2-3 times your loan payment)
- How long you have been Employed in the 'same type of job'

If you can provide proof of all this and can meet these requirements, then you should have no problem whatsoever in obtaining your loan.

HOW DO I PICK A REALTOR?

The Realtor you end up choosing is going to be in charge of your greatest asset: your home. You would do well to make sure you ask the right questions and interview a Realtor properly. Here are some questions you may consider asking:

- How much experience do they have?
- Are they a member of the association of Realtors?
- Do they show enthusiasm or are they zombies?
- Did they explain everything to you in detail?
- Did they bring comparable data?
- Do they have an Active Realtor license?
- What have they sold lately?

What about those Real Estate Companies that will sell your home for only a 2% commission instead of the usual 6%?

Here is how some of them work. The ‘Low-cost’ Realty Company will promise you that you, the Seller will only have to pay a very small commission for their Agent to sell your home. Of course, you jump right on it hoping to save 4% (on a $100,000 home, a 4% in savings is $4000)!

The truth is that in order to save any real money, there are certain things that you are required to do by yourself, **such as showing your own home to every buyer that wants to take a look**! If you do not do this, you can expect to tack on an additional 2% to the Agent's commission, thereby making their entire commission 4%.

On top of this, if another Realtor from a different Broker sells your home, a co-brokerage fee of an additional 2% will be paid to that Realtor.

For most Homeowners, they will try to show the house themselves. After some time, most people will give up due to frustration, inexperience, and lost personal time. The Realtor then takes over and your additional 2% is added to your starting 2%. From here, you have a 50/50 shot that a different Realtor than the one you hired will sell your home!

Once everything is said and done, you are paying the entire 6% that the Broker said you wouldn't have to pay. Take it from me – just hire the best Broker you can afford at a good price and forget about 'cheating the system'.

HOW TO MARKET A PRODUCT OR YOUR BUSINESS SUCCESSFULLY:

- Join a Business Referral Group in your area
- Publish & distribute a free Newsletter

- Write & publish articles online or in print
- Build a Website
- Use SEO (Search Engine Optimization)
- Submit your Website to search engines, directories, and print the web address on business cards
- Create & send E-mail Newsletters
- Build an E-mail Database
- Make a 1 page list of References
- Ask for Referrals from Clients
- Donate services or products to media outlets (radio, tv, etc), connected people, and silent auctions
- Send out as many press releases as you can (you can even do this online for free or low cost)
- Hold a family or informational Event at a park
- Create, print out and pass out Flyers

- Mail out 'Discount' Postcards (Postcards are much cheaper than regular mail)
- Leave a business card wherever you go; even at rest stops, vacation homes, hotel rooms, etc. Someone will find it and possibly take a look
- Offer a free product, discount, or service
- Ask current Clients if you can put up a business card holder with your information
- Barter your services
- Co-advertise with another business
- Believe in your product or service

How to have the best odds at getting a loan from the Bank:

- Have a Good & Clean Credit History
- Your chances are better if you already have a history with the Bank; start with your own Bank or Credit Union

- Your chances are better if you have already had one loan with the bank and Paid It Back

- Have the Information the Bank will Need already prepared

- Have the Loan Officer add back the depreciation you took out on company equipment (Business Owners); this way, you show a higher income

- Pay everything possible through your Business so any debts that show up on your Business are not counted against you Personally (Business Owners)

- No matter what – Be Polite

The Difference Between Banks and Credit Unions:

  - Credit Unions are Non-profits**
  - Credit Unions usually have lower interest rates
  - Banks are usually Nationwide; most Credit Unions are not – however some C.U. now have Networks (other Nationwide Partners) where their same rules apply
  - Some Credit Unions are not insured
  - Banks have a larger ATM network

CHAPTER 8

The Truth About FISH:

This is a question that does not come up as often as it should. Everyone knows that fish is good for you; who knew that it can also be hazardous to your health? All fish contain mercury, but some are safer to eat and some you should just stay away from.

Mercury can have negative health affects and cause permanent damage to major organs such as your brain, lungs, and kidneys! Most importantly, it can severely affect a **developing fetus**.

Brain Damage, Mental Retardation, Blindness, and even Cancer have been a direct result of Mercury Poisoning. Mercury is listed by the Government as the **third most toxic chemical known to man**. Pregnant Women & Small Children should avoid all but the lowest level. Even then, eat no more than 2 servings per week.

DO NOT EAT (highest levels of mercury):

- Shark
- Orange Roughy
- Marlin
- Swordfish

- Tilefish
- Ahi Tuna

ADVISED TO EAT SPARINGLY (high levels):

- Bluefish
- Grouper
- Sea Bass
- Albacore & Yellowfin Tuna

EAT FEWER (moderate levels):

- Tuna (chunk light/canned)
- Cod
- Halibut
- Carp
- Lobster
- Bass
- Mahi Mahi
- Monkfish
- Perch
- Snapper

SAFER TO EAT (lower levels):

- Crab
- Clams

- Crawfish
- Anchovies
- Flounder
- Haddock
- Herring
- Mackerel
- Mullet
- Oysters
- Salmon
- Sardines
- Scallops
- Shrimp
- Sole
- Squid
- Tilapia
- Trout
- Whitefish
- Perch
- Pollock

Most of you are probably wondering how to get the benefits of all those Omega-3 fatty acids if you shouldn't eat most fish, right? For the most part, **Fish Oil Capsules** are a safer alternative! 1,000-2,000 Mgs daily should provide all the benefits without the additional risk.

CHAPTER 9

HOW CAN I PROTECT MY PC?

If you are like me, you do most everything on your computer: media, communication, and entertainment. Viruses, Malware, and Spyware are the worst things to happen in the digital age and continue to be a hindrance to everyday life.

Luckily for you, I happen to own a computer company and I am going to give you some free hints to keep your computer protected!

The most important things to know are –

- Don't Be Stupid! Don't **open emails** from people you don't know. Stay away from unrecognized video/audio/**attachments**.

- Don't allow people to **transfer files** from their Flash Drives to your PC without scanning the files first with Antivirus/Anti-spyware software.

- Be very careful of **Peer to Peer Networks** such as Limewire & Bearshare; there is no telling what you may get and the chance of infection is very high.

- Make sure you have Antivirus & Antispyware/Malware; there is no excuse whatsoever for not having these. Especially when you can get them for **free!**

- Use your **Firewall**! A Firewall blocks your open Ports and can Filter Packets.

- **If you get a **Pop-up** that says ‘your computer is infected by viruses’ and asks if you would like to ‘initiate a scan or remove the viruses’, use your head! Is it completely different from the programs you know you have? If so, it’s a **Virus** and you should use **Task Manager** (Ctrl,Alt,Del) to close down the Internet Page. Open a new Internet Explorer page and clear your **Cache**.

- **Do Not** place anything **Magnetic** or that causes **static electricity/friction** near or on your computer!

HOW TO BOOST COMPUTER SPEEDS:

Everyone has had this happen: you buy a new desktop or laptop and it is lightening fast. However, during the months, you notice that things are starting to slow down. In fact, sometimes it takes almost a minute to simply open up a program. Here are a few tips to keep this from happening:

- The larger the files you have (music, video, games), the bigger Hard Drive you need.
- Empty your Recycle Bin once a week; files are never deleted from the hard drive until you do.
- Try not to over-use Shortcuts; they take up significant RAM.
- Remove files from RAM by refreshing the Desktop after you close out of a program.
- Delete Cookies and Temporary Internet Files at least once a week.
- Use 'Msconfig' (Click 'Start' button & type msconfig) to keep un-needed programs from starting up automatically.
- Use 2 different Partitions: 1 for larger programs & the other for music/video/games storage.
- Keep your computer Dust free!

- Defrag your Hard Drive at least once every 2-3 months.

HOW TO DOWNLOAD VIDEOS FROM YOUTUBE:

Have you noticed yet that you cannot simply right-click and save a YouTube video (at least using Internet Explorer)? So what happens if you see a really cool video and want to save it to watch later? Follow this guide to find out how:

Go to www.youtube.com and find your favorite video you've always wanted to download.

- In the Address Bar highlight the Link, right-click and **Copy** it.

- Open another Internet Explorer Tab and type in: www.Keepvid.com.

- Right-click and **Paste** the Link.

- Click on '**Download**' button and a Link pops up

- Click on the Link & **Save** the File to your Desktop or a New Folder.

- Once File is saved, right-click on it and Rename it as a **'.flv'** type file.

- Download the free **FLV Player** from www.Keepvid.com and relax, kick back, and watch your favorite Video anytime you want!

MONEY-SAVING FREE SOFTWARE:

Okay – as most of you know, a long time ago, in a galaxy far, far away, Microsoft was once a benevolent entity. They used to offer Microsoft Office for free with a new desktop PC. Fast forward to the future and Microsoft Office now costs between $200 and $400! Whatever are we to do now? Here is a guide to some great FREE software:

Open Office: www.openoffice.org – go here and download an open-source software package that is 100% compatible with Microsoft Office! What does that mean? It means that you can send, receive, open, & edit Microsoft Documents without paying the ridiculous prices for them! Here is how the Open Office programs Mix & Match with Microsoft Office:

- Writer = Word
- Calc = Excel
- Impress = Powerpoint

- Base = Access
- Draw = Visio
- Math = Equation Editor

Need a free Antivirus? Try **Avast**: www.avast.com

Need a free Anti-spyware? Try **Windows Defender**: www.microsoft.com and search for it.

Need a free Anti-malware? Try **Malwarebytes**: www.malwarebytes.com

Want a free Firewall that will beat Windows Firewall any day? Try **Zone Alarm**: www.zonealarm.com

Need a Website, but can't afford to hire a Designer? Try **Weebly**: www.weebly.com

Want to make free calls over the Internet? Try **Skype**: www.skype.com

Need some free Photo Editing Software? Try **Photoscape**: www.photoscape.org

Need to Encrypt your Files or keep your Data from Prying Eyes? Try **TrueCrypt**: www.truecrypt.org

I'm just going to throw this one in there. Do you want to make a great impression with full color Business Cards? Would you like to get them for 'pennies on the dollar'? Try **Iprint**: www.iprint.com

HOW TO RECOVER YOUR DATA:

What happens if your Hard Drive crashes and you lose all your important pictures, videos, school work, or other critical data? Is it really gone or is there a way to recover it?

There are a few ways to know that your Hard Drive is going to crash. The most common ones are:

- Regular Blue Screens or other Computer Crashes, such as sudden shut-downs
- Strange Sounds such as loud grinding or disk interruptions
- Your C: Drive Letter disappears
- Longer than usual time to access programs

**If any of these signs are there, STOP everything you are doing and do a Data Backup! You do not have time to waste!

So what happens if the drive crashes or is inaccessible? There are a few things you can try yourself to recover your data before going with the last resort of calling a Professional:

- Remove your Hard Drive and put it in the Freezer for a few hours. Reconnect it and see if it works. If it does, save as much data because most likely, it will be the last chance you have.

- Remove your Hard Drive and connect it to an External Drive Enclosure. You can use the USB to hook it up to another computer and save the data on the main drive.

- Download and use a Ubuntu Boot CD: www.ubuntu.com/GetUbuntu/download. Download the ISO image to your local Hard Drive and then burn it onto a CD (**it must be a CD**, not a DVD). Put the CD into the disk drive and reboot your computer. Follow the directions to access your data.

HOW TO NAVIGATE YOUR COMPUTER WHEN YOUR MOUSE STOPS WORKING:

Now, most likely, this won't happen to you so not much to worry about, right? Actually, it's more common than you think. Here is how you can navigate even without your mouse:

1. Activate '**Mousekeys**' by holding pressing **SHIFT** + **ALT** + **NUM LOCK** at the same time.

2. Got into '**Settings**' and adjust mouse speed, pointer speed, and screen status to your preferences.

3. **Navigate** your computer by using these buttons on your numeric keypad –

    - **8 Key** moves up
    - **2 Key** moves down
    - **4 Key** moves left
    - **6 Key** moves right
    - **5 Key** clicks on something
    - **+ (Plus) Sign** is double-click
    - **- (Minus) Sign** is right-click

- **Insert Key** to hold & drag
- **Delete Key** to release

Fastest Fix for Loss of Internet Connection:
Reboot your Cable Modem! Unplug it from the wall for about 30 seconds to allow it to refresh.

Useful Websites (that you may not have known about):

www.lifehacker.com – Need a question answered or information found? This is the place to go.

www.howstuffworks.com - How most everything works!

www.homefair.com – Do you have questions on moving, career, or family?

www.epinions.com – A Free 'Consumer-reports' type Site.

www.cnet.com – Find Product Reviews/Prices, Software Downloads, and more.

www.pandora.com –Create, build, and listen to your own music station!

www.rifeo.com – Get free music lessons from Musicians!

CHAPTER 10

WHAT PERSONAL EXPENSES CAN YOU WRITE OFF IF YOU OWN A BUSINESS:

This is an interesting question with a rather long answer. The first thing is assuming you own a Business. The second thing is if you want to show a Profit for the Business or if you want to keep more money for yourself and not have to pay more in taxes.

The easiest ways to do this is to use Business Monies to pay for anything you may think is Business-related. These are also 'Write-offs' for the Business as well so you both come out ahead!

- Phones, Cell Phones, & Pagers
- Computers: desktops & laptops
- Internet Expenses
- Electronics that have a Business use
- Newspapers, Magazines, & Books
- Meals & Entertainment

- Vehicle Repairs
- Gas or Fuel for a Vehicle/Equipment
- Mileage to Business-related events
- Medical/Dental Insurance
- Medical/Medicine Out of Pocket Expenses
- Recreational Vehicles
- Gifts

WHAT HAPPENS TO YOU ONCE YOU QUIT SMOKING:

This is really quite amazing to know and it may even help you quit! I quit cold turkey one day when I took a Lung Quality test at the local YMCA. I waited in line with a bunch of grade school kids and I failed miserably! The nurse told me that the score was well below normal and I should get to a doctor fast. Hopefully with this information, you won't wait as long as I did. Here are the changes that take place in your body after you stop smoking:

- Within 20 minutes, your blood pressure, pulse rate, and body temperature drop & increase to normal levels.

- Within 8 hours, the Carbon Monoxide level in your blood drops to normal and your Oxygen level increases to normal.

- Within 24 hours, your chances of having a heart attack decrease!

- Within 48 hours, all nicotine in your body will have left and your senses of touch and smell will return to normal.

- Within 72 hours, your energy levels will increase and your bronchial tubes will relax.

- Within 2 weeks through the next 3 months, your circulation will improve, breathing becomes easier, and lung function increases to 30%.

- Within the next 6 months, respiratory discomfort, coughing, congestion, tiredness, and shortness of breath will decrease. Your lungs will begin to re-grow.

- Within 13 months, your risk of heart disease becomes half that of a smoker.

- Within 5 years, your risk for lung cancer decreases to almost half, stroke risk is reduced to that of a non-smoker, and risk of mouth, throat, & esophagus cancer comes down by almost half.

- Within 10 years, most risks of disease that you had while smoking are now similar with that of non-smokers and precancerous cells are replaced.

- Within 15 years, risk of heart disease is now that of a non-smoker.

Now, if all these reasons are simply not enough for you to quit smoking, then listen carefully. I've been told so many times what horrible things may occur if I didn't stop smoking. I didn't listen.

What I did find out was that if I were told what the good things that can happen to me if I were to quit, I would have probably done it sooner. Besides all of the above, I will tell you from personal experience that you can be there to do so much more with your family and children and that is worth its weight in gold. Good Luck!

HOW TO TIE A TIE:

This is a must-know for any man – period. Obviously, there are many ways to tie a tie, but for this book, we will use the most used one. So, put your tie around your neck and face the mirror.

1. Make sure the Wider End is on your right side and about 10-12 inches further down than the left side.

2. Now cross the Wide End over the Small End to form a kind of triangle.

3. Bring the Wide End underneath the Small End and up towards your Upper Left.

4. Wrap the Wide End back over the Small End towards your Center Right.

5. **You will now have a Knot.

6. Bring the Wide End under the Knot and up towards your face.

7. Hold the front of the Knot lightly while bringing the Wide End down and through the Front Loop.

8. Using one hand, pull the Small End down while using the other hand to hold the Knot and move it up.

HOW TO AVOID SPEED TRAPS:

Now, obviously I'm not telling you to jump in your car and go 90 miles an hour; speeding is dangerous and is no joke. This is simply for those who are careful drivers, but are wary of keeping up with traffic. This amazing site will show you where the most common speed traps are in your city and state:
http://www.speedtrap.org

HOW TO SELF-PUBLISH A BOOK:

Did you know that some statistics say that 80-85% of people would love to write a book? Many of them have never taken the first steps towards their goals simply because of one reason: they don't know how to go about doing it. If the information were out there, would the percentage of people who follow through with their dreams change? Let's find out.

The first thing you need is a great **Story**. Whether it is fiction or non-fiction, it doesn't matter – just go with what you feel comfortable with. Every one of you is a storyteller; most of you just don't know it yet. Once we have a story or some type of factual documentation finished, you can then proceed with the **Editing**.

Most Writers do a terrible job of editing their own work so either hire a professional or let someone who is in a similar profession handle it. Perhaps your English Professor or a neighborhood Journalist can help those who are low on funds. Trust me; I've made these mistakes before.

An Editor's job is to edit and proofread a manuscript. They will check for proper prose and grammar. Some will even tell you how to improve your story or even do the fact-checking for some non-fiction works. Margins, fonts, chapter headings, and indexes should all be correct before proceeding.

Now that you are finished with all the tedious manipulations, you must choose a size for your book and edit it again! There are many Industry Standard Sizes for your book, but we will just focus on the three most common ones:

5.5 x 8.5 – Paperback Book

7 x 10 – Informational Book

8 x 10 – Hardcover Book

The next step is your **Cover**. This is undoubtedly one of the most important parts of your book. It is what decides if a random person browsing through a bookstore picks up your book or doesn't. The Cover needs to be attractive or unique enough to hold their attention.

If you are 'Art Adept', feel free to design it yourself. If, however, you have no creativity in your bones for art or design, find someone who does! Regardless of how you do it, please make sure that the Cover complements the inner workings of the book. Don't have a picture of an interstellar galactic space war on the Cover and the book be about Butterflies!

Many types of Design Software is out there as well. I personally use a program called BookCover Pro: http://www.bookcoverpro.com/. This Site also has an E-book cover creator and a program called: PrintMarketingPro that may come in handy for you. Either way, it is your choice. Remember to leave at least a 2-2.5" open box area on the lower right-hand corner of the cover. This is where your ISBN & Barcode will be set.

Now, to make sure the book and the cover are the correct size and we do not end up with a much larger cover that swallows the book, we must do some math. Here is an easy website you can use to determine the correct **cover/spine** size you will need: http://www.lulu.com/en/includes/calc_spine_inc.php or to calculate the spine width (in inches) **manually**, follow this guide:

Non-color Books:

Paper Weight of 60lbs (White Paper): # of pages x 0.00225

Paper Weight of 70lbs (Cream Paper): # of pages x 0.0025

Color Books:

Paper Weight of 80lbs (**Matte**): # of pages x 0.0024

Paper Weight of 80lbs (**Gloss**): # of pages x 0.0021

Paper Weight of 100lbs (Matte): # of pages x 0.0032

Paper Weight of 100lbs (Gloss): # of pages x 0.0028

**For some Publishing Companies, these calculations may vary slightly

Some Authors like to decorate the Spine of the book with designs and pictures, and this is completely fine. In fact, this technique can make your book stand out from the rest; especially for people browsing the library aisles. However, if you are writing a book with less than 100 pages, a blank spine is strongly recommended. The spine will be too small to fit anything legible on.

Okay – now that we are done with this, we'll continue on to the Intricacies of making the book yours. What do I mean by that? No one wants to have their ideas, story, or works stolen or copied. In order to protect our book we need to **copyright** it. You can do this online by using this website: www.eco.copyright.gov. Copyrighting your book will grant you exclusive rights to license, transfer, or assign your works. *ISBN, Bar Code, & LCCN **before** copyright!

An **ISBN Number** is a 10-digit (now a 13-digit) number that is a unique identifier for your book. It is used to establish & identify a title of one specific publisher. It also allows you to efficiently market your book to retail outlets, libraries, and distributors. You can get your ISBN number from Bowker Identifier Services: www.myidentifiers.com and your **Bar Code** at the same site. Large book retailers and wholesalers require you to have a barcode to sell your book.

At this point, you will have to figure out a Price for your book. If you want it to sell it quickly and numbers matter to you, you may just consider pricing it a bit below standard retail prices. Of course, if you know that the book will have such a dramatic impact on humanity and people will pay to get their hands on it, then by all means, price it higher than usual.

An **LCCN** (Library of Congress Catalog Number) will allow Libraries nationwide to order and catalog your book. The LCCN is printed on the bottom portion of your book. You can register to get one online as well: **http://pcn.loc.gov.**

Whew….what a pain, right?! You can relax now because we are done with most of the mental work. Now we need an outlet to create, print, and distribute your book. There are many out there nowadays, but I use **Create Space**: **www.createspace.com**. This online publishing Site will allow you to do most of your printing, distributing, and marketing right from there. They distribute your book through **Amazon** and **Target** (online only).

Before Publishing, you may want to register for a CIP (Cataloging In Publication) Data Block here: http://cip.loc.gov

The last thing you will need to do is to **market** your book to the general public. There are many outlets that you can use to advertise and make your book known:

- Social Networks: Facebook, MySpace, Etc.
- Create & Design a Website
- Solicit your local Library or Book Store to stock it or sell it on their shelves; they may expect a small fee
- Online Forums: Tell People about your book
- Most Book Sites have Community Forums that allow you to tell other Members about your book

- Word of Mouth: Family, Friends, Co-workers, Whoever will listen
- Flyers in local Book Stores/Grocery Stores
- Purchase some colorful Business Cards with your Book Information on it, especially the Website
- Build an Online Presence
- Send a Press Release online or to your local newspaper

****Something Very Important to remember** – If you sign on with a company that **gives** you an ISBN, **make sure** that you still own all of your rights to the book!

Here is a small breakdown of the costs associated with writing, publishing, and printing a book:

- The **ISBN** Number only is $125.00
- The ISBN Number + **Bar Code** is $150.00
- A **20 Pack** of ISBN Numbers only is $250.00
- A **Single** Bar Code is $25.00
- To **Copyright** your Book **Online** is $35.00
- To **Copyright** your Book by **Mail** is $50.00

- There is no cost to obtain an **LCCN**, however, you must mail a complimentary copy of your book immediately after publication
- There is no cost to obtain a CIP, however you must get it before you publish your book & also mail a complimentary copy
- It will cost you between $10 & $20 to purchase a **Domain Name** for your Website
- It will cost around $5 to $25 a month to **Host** your Website with a reputable company
- If you go with **Createspace** as your Book Distributor, I urge you to purchase the Pro Plan for $39.00 + a $5 Annual Fee – this will allow you to get increased **Royalties** per sale / any copies of your book are discounted
- If you do a News or Press Release, the cost will be around $200+ - **There are Sites out there that may do this for free
- Printing Business Cards in full color will only cost around $20 for 250 if you go with Iprint.com
- Paper and Ink will cost around $30-$50 total for advertising flyers, sample prints, & marketing material; the rest is up to you

Note that each **book bar code price has a **'5'** in front of it. The '5' is a code for the **US Dollar**. For example, **51495** means **$14.95** – Interesting, huh?

Fast Guide to Drive a Stick-Shift:

1. There are 3 pedals: Clutch, Brake, & Gas
2. Keep Clutch down each time you Shift Gears
3. Slowly press on the Gas Pedal as you continue to release the Clutch
4. Each time you hit 3,000 rpm's, take your foot off the Gas, press down on the Clutch, & pull the Gearshift to the next Gear
5. Release the Clutch gently, while pressing the Gas Pedal at the same time
6. Decrease your speed by releasing the Gas Pedal, press down on the Clutch, and Shift to next Gear
7. Release the Clutch as you keep foot on gas
8. If going in Reverse, let the Clutch out slowly using the brake if needed
9. **Important**: Always remember to use the Emergency Brake when parking as there is no 'park' gear on a stick

Lastly, to gratuitously take up space & waste some of your precious time, please proceed to:

HOW TO SURVIVE A ZOMBIE ATTACK:

You just never know when a Zombie Outbreak will start so I'm going to run through this very quickly. First of all, Zombie's are gross and disgusting; they are cannibals; and lucky for you – they are extremely stupid!

The most important thing to do right now is to go to your local grocery store and pick up roughly $10,000 in canned, non-spoiling foods. You may also want to get a Can Opener. For those who cannot cook, there's not much difference here, but for the rest of you – get used to eating this crap. Take all of it and stock it in –preferably – an underground bomb shelter. Otherwise, just keep it under your bed or somewhere nice & dark.

Walmart would be the best place to go because you can also pick up a chainsaw, a firearm, waterproof matches, a flashlight, and a first aid kit.

Now go back to your shelter, hope and pray that no undead ghouls ever find you and be prepared to shoot or cut off their heads if they do. It's the only way to kill a zombie! Unfortunately for you, you will most likely not survive the night.

Luckily, you have this book to throw at them when you run out of ammo (after you've read it, of course). Remember: whether you are dead or alive by the end of the night, you will have gathered a wealth of knowledge that you can make use of in this life or the next!

**This book is dedicated to my Family:

My Father, Neil Kumaraperu; My Mother, Indrani Kumaraperu; My Brother, Raji Kumaraperu; My Sister, Amy Kumaraperu; My many Aunts & Uncles, Cousins, and everyone in-between; My Wife, Sarah Kumaraperu; and my amazing Children: Ethan, Cain, Cyerra, Sydney, and Ashlynn; two of whom are on the Cover!

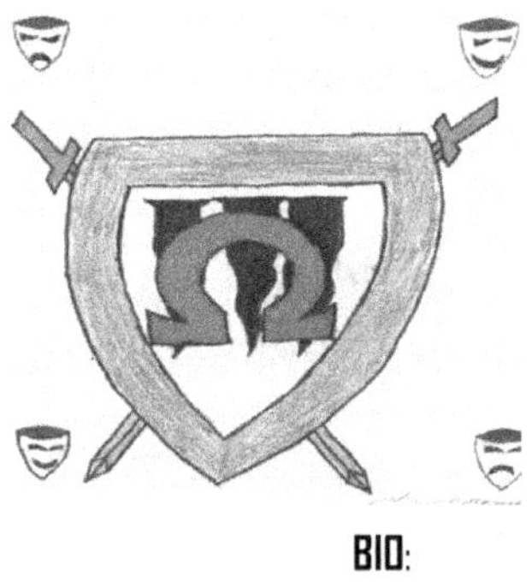

BIO:

Nishan Kumaraperu is an aspiring Author who is also the owner of CNR Enterprises Inc. (together with his partner). Although he considers himself an Amateur, he has had his works praised by many; criticized by some, and even large rocks thrown at him by a few well-intentioned psychopaths. Even though he finds it a chore to write his own short Bio for this book, he persists in gratifying his audience. The smoke alarm is going off now which means his dinner is almost ready, yet he will not eat a bite until this statement to his life is finished. Many have said that Kumaraperu's commitment to his audience is utterly amazing and so far....I would have to agree. People have agreed that he is not French, nor is he from France; however, he will leave you now with this single unpronounceable, yet fancy French word: **Adieu**

WWW.HELPYOURSELFBOOK.COM

www.ingramcontent.com/pod-product-compliance
Lightning Source LLC
LaVergne TN
LVHW020649100826
845148LV00012B/2397

* 9 7 8 0 6 1 5 3 6 7 0 6 4 *